Victim to VIC'

By

Sarah Champion

RB
Rossendale Books

Published by Rossendale Books

11 MowgrainView, Bacup,
Rossendale, Lancashire
OL13 8EJ
England

Published in paperback 2012

ISBN 978-1-4717-7577-2

Copyright Sarah Champion 2012

All rights reserved. No part of this publication may be reproduced, stored in a retrieval system, or in any form or by any means, without the prior permission in writing of the publisher, nor be otherwise circulated in any form of binding or cover other than that in which it is published and without a similar condition including this condition being imposed on the subsequent purchaser.

Dedication

This book is dedicated to my husband, who has been so loving and patient with me.

He has walked the recent part of my journey with me.

He is not only my husband but also my best friend.

He is such an example of true humility and love.

A quiet man but a spiritual giant.

Acknowledgments

I want to thank my husband for being so understanding for the many times a pizza rather than a delicious pasta meal has appeared on his dinner plate because I have been holed up for hours at a time with this book.

Thanks to Charlynne Boddie who was the first person to read the raw copy of this book and offer her advice and constructive criticism.

To my friends too many to name –you know who you are - who have encouraged me on, and loved me through the difficult times.

To my children who have forgiven me and love me.

Introduction

While I was still quite young I wondered how I would be able to help other women who had been through some if not all of the things I had been through, or who still had to suffer in one way or another.

Sexual abuse, miscarriages, stillbirth, hysterectomy, multiple operations, poverty, desertion, deaths, rejection and road traffic accidents are just some things I have suffered.

It never occurred to me that I would ever write a book about it all. Once the decision was made though, all at once it made sense of what has been such a difficult life.

Through it all God has sustained me, protected me and most of all loved me. When I had sunk into the depths of shame, He was still there.

When my back was turned against Him, He never gave up on me. My prayer and desire is that as you read this book you too will find wholeness and joy from the only one who can give it to you.

Our Daddy... the one who will never let you down or hurt you. The one who is always with you. The one who loves you with a love like no other.

Sarah Champion

Contents

Chapter 1 9
A Planned Birth

Chapter 2 16
A New Family

Chapter 3 22
A Different Life

Chapter 4 29
A New Man

Chapter 5 36
Lost Children

Chapter 6 46
An Old Love

Chapter 7 53
A New Way

Chapter 8 59
A New Life

Chapter 9 68
A New Union

Chapter 10 80
A New Home

Chapter 11 89
A New Career

EPILOGUE 100

Chapter 1

A Planned Birth

Before I formed you in the womb, I knew you, and before you were born, I consecrated you; I appointed you…
Jeremiah Chapter 1 verse 5

For many years now, I have felt the need to write my story in the hope that it will help and encourage others who are facing or have faced similar experiences to mine, but it's only now that I have felt free enough to put pen to paper.

This is a testimony of what God can do in the life of a broken, abused, insecure person.

It has taken quite a lot of ministry to get to the place that I now find myself. That place of total FREEDOM. Free from all that tormented me and held me back from being the person God intended me to be. So here is my story, which because of God's amazing grace and emotional healing has become HIS STORY.

Whenever I start reading a book, I always wonder

how the author decided how to begin? I too faced this dilemma, but in the words of Julie Andrews in the sound of music… "let's start at the very beginning".

I was born into a very dysfunctional family. Of course, I did not realise this straight away but as the years went on it became very apparent. My parents told me repeatedly that I was an accident and I imagine many of you have been told the same.

I was fostered out to various 'friends' of my parents. My father was an alcoholic, a violent one at that. My mother had to work full time to bring any money in. They had no time to care for a baby that they did not even want!

I was placed with a neighbour who lived opposite, but at 6 weeks old, I contracted whooping cough so my neighbour swiftly handed me back as she could not cope with the responsibility.

Following that, I was placed with three other unofficial foster carers but none worked out for one reason or another.

Then my mother asked her cousin who lived in

the next town if she would care for me. She approached her, confident that she would take me on as she had two older children of her own. Of course, there would be some remuneration in it for her.

With her husband away in the navy, the money would after all come in very useful! Particularly as she liked to drink.

We shall call her Sylvia. She was a hard brash Irish woman, and my only memories of her are of a cruel vindictive woman.

This is where my first memories come in. I was about two years old. One night I remember feeling very sick, and when I called out to her, she scolded me and ordered me to go back to sleep. Upon that, I was violently sick over the bed - this caused her to fly into one of her rages that had become all too frequent, I was petrified of her.

She used to love tying me up. Usually it was to the old gas cooker in the kitchen.

The final memory I have of my time there was once again being tied up, but this time it was on the front doorstep, to one of those 'H' shaped metal things that people used to wipe their boots or shoes on. Sylvia had gone out leaving me alone!

While I was sitting there, still in my pyjamas - a man approached me asking how long I had been there. As I was only about two years old I had no idea. I remember that I started to cry. He untied me, which gave me even more fear than I already had. He took me on a bus; I recall it seeming a very long journey. (I was to find out years later that this man was my father.)

My next memory is that of living with an aunty and uncle. His father was my maternal grandmother's brother. He lived in the house also.

I wanted for nothing materially during my time with them. Nothing except safety. You see my uncle started abusing me during my time there. He was an ex-chief petty officer in the navy and ruled the home as I can only imagine he used to rule his crew. I hated the way he spoke to my aunty, he had a particularly cruel tone to his voice, one that has remained with me and caused me years of insecurity and fear.

For years, I was convinced that my aunty was unaware of what he was doing to me, but as I have grown older and hopefully wiser, I now feel that she may indeed have known but was powerless to do anything about it.

We did not have all the support groups for abused children, battered wives etc. that we now have. I am not suggesting that my aunty was battered, but as I came to learn later on, many times, a physical beating is preferable to verbal abuse. At least it is finished quickly, whereas verbal abuse just goes on and on relentlessly.

I lived with them until I was 11 years old. I felt the odd one out at school as all the other children referred to their mum and dad and laughed when I said that I never knew mine! I was also dressed differently to them as my aunty was very old-fashioned and that was reflected in the way she dressed me. Never the less I adored her.

Life was dominated by routine, my uncle's routine that is. Breakfast was at the same time every day. Each day a hooter would sound from the factory where my uncle worked and that would signal lunchtime. He would walk home so we could all have a dinner together.
Five o clock was teatime. Every day we had sand-

wiches of one variety or another followed by a piece of my auntie's homemade cake.

Eight o'clock was suppertime. Jacobs cream crackers and a piece of cheese. It had to be the correct cheese though. My uncle made sure of that, as he did all the shopping. He would make my aunty stay at home while he did it.

Friday night was bath night. We did not have a plumbed-in bath, so a large metal bathtub was brought in from the shed and filled with hot water. There was a strict pecking order though.

First in was my uncle, then his father. Following that my aunty and finally me. By the time I got in, the bath was full of scum. There were no nice shower gels in those days! The bar of lifebuoy soap left awful scum on the surface so I usually emerged with a ring of this around my midriff.

Evenings were one of the worst times for me. After tea, my uncle used to put his car away in a garage block, which was a few minutes' walk from the house. He always insisted I come with him. Once there he would mess around with me touching me in inappropriate areas.
My bed was in the same bedroom as them and I

dreaded the time when I had to retire for the night. As young as I was, I longed to die.

I did enjoy the times alone with my aunty though. She would spoil me with treats that I was never allowed to have when my uncle was there. She was my world. I felt safe with her.

Chapter 2

A New Family

Know for certain that your family will be strangers...
Genesis chapter 15 verse 13a

One day my world was shattered when my aunty told me that I had to leave them to go and live with my 'mum and dad'. I had never used that word in my vocabulary before, as it had become a way of life to talk at school about my aunty!

Years later, I discovered that my parents wanted a council house at that time so they told the local authority that they had three children as well as my maternal grandmother living with them. On the strength of that they were given a four bed roomed house, albeit in one of the most atrocious council estates just a short journey from the town center. This was a shock in itself because whatever else was happening in the home, my aunty and uncle lived in a quiet middle class area.

Shortly after that warning, a tall skinny boy, much older than me, came to my auntie's house to take me away. I did not know at the time that he was my brother and was actually seven years older than I was.

We had a long walk to my new home, and the journey was spent with him telling me that we had a 'Nan' who lived with them who had a fierce dog that hated little girls, and would bite them whenever she saw one!

On arriving, I discovered I also had a sister, she was eight years older. It was immediately obvious that my brother and sister were very close. The dog turned out to be a Scottish terrier who although he barked and yapped constantly (or so it seemed) did not bite me. So all the fear that had built up inside me on that long walk was in fact built on a lie.

It soon became apparent that my sister and brother hated me. They did not like this little intruder one bit. Apart from anything else, I spoke differently to them. I had to talk properly whilst with my uncle, as he used to sit me down often, teaching elocution to me. This did not make me popular in the neighborhood I now found myself living in, which, was described as a hard, working class area.

After a couple of nights in my new home, I experienced the greatest of shocks when my father tried to strangle my mother. I had never witnessed physical violence before and all I could do was stand and scream in the corner of the room. I was shaking so violently that I thought I was dying.

My sister hit me and told me to help her in trying to get my father away from my mother. After several hard hits from my father, he eventually stopped and released my mother. Her eye was black and her nose was bleeding. I was terrified and once again wanted to die. I could not imagine living the rest of my childhood in this place.

One day on coming home from school, I walked into the garden and before I knew, what was happening my brother threw a knife at me whilst calling me awful names. My sister stood by laughing. I was becoming desperate. I had never known such unhappiness and fear.

A year or so after I moved in my father sent my brother to live with one of his sisters in America; my brother was getting in with a bad Teddy Boy crowd. My father thought it would introduce him to a better way of living.

He was only seventeen years old and understandably did not want to go. My father told him that if he did not go he would beat my mother up longer and harder than he did at present!

I was pleased as now I only had my sister to contend with, and thought that with my brother out of the way she would be kinder to me. I was wrong!

Due to my father being an alcoholic, it meant the physical violence was a regular occurrence. My mum worked full time and dad drank the money away. One day while my dad was at work, a police officer came to our front door to inform my sister and me that he had fallen from a ladder at work and was in hospital.

It transpired that he was drunk as usual and had fallen from the ladder breaking his back in the process.

When he was finally discharged from hospital, he was unable to work. Fortunately, the surgery he had undergone was successful in as much as he could walk and live a fairly normal life. At the same time, this was the worst news I could have received. It meant he was at home all the time.

I dreaded coming home from school; I used to stand almost frozen at the front door whilst trying to get my key in the lock. It was difficult because I would always start shaking uncontrollably. The house reeked of cigarettes and alcohol - whiskey to be precise. He was always, without exception, aggressive when he had been drinking.

At the top of the road, there was a pub, which my parents frequented most nights. I always had to go with them and sit outside waiting. On one particular night when we were walking back home, dad started beating my mum up throwing her into the hedges and punching her really badly, there was blood everywhere, I was terrified.

In those days, there were still police officers on the beat so I ran and ran until I found one. I pleaded with him to arrest my dad but as he followed me to where it was happening he told me it was classed as a 'domestic' and they could not intervene! I could not believe I was hearing this!

Who was going to help me get out of the nightmare life I was being forced to live in? One night after I had gone to bed, I started planning how I could kill my dad. I knew it was a certainty that he would start being violent with my mum again the next night so I planned to do it then. I was convinced that I would not be arrested, as it would be seen as self-defense. Besides, I was a child.

Sure enough the next night he started hitting my mum again, this time he had her in a strangle hold against the kitchen door. I grabbed a flimsy brass toasting fork that used to hang by the fireplace, and I started stabbing him in the arm of all places… I will never forget that night. He turned to look at me, he still had one hand around mum's neck and with an almighty swipe of his other hand, he lashed out throwing me to the other side of the room.

How silly I was to have thought that such a small insignificant object could in any way stop a powerfully strong Irish man.

The years passed by and I constantly pleaded with my mum to leave him, but she explained that there would be nowhere to go. I mentioned previously that there were no shelters in those days, no phone help lines, nothing!

Chapter 3

A Different Life

...and you are of Christ...
1 Corinthians chapter 3 verse 23

When I was twelve, I developed a love for classical music and starting learning any musical instrument I could get my hands on at school. I played the violin, recorder, cello and piano and dabbled in several more. My music teacher was a kind compassionate woman and I learnt so much from her. As I could not afford any instruments of my own, she managed to get a violin and a piano for me; I have no idea to this day where they came from.

On returning home from school, I always had chores to do around the house, my sister had married and I was now the only one left, but once these were completed, I hid myself away in the spare front room to practice. I would get lost in my music and it became a wonderful escape.

On parents' evenings or school concerts, I used

to look around expectantly, hoping my parents would be there to see how well I was doing and to see me moving from one instrument to another during the concerts, but they were never there.

When I was fourteen, the music teacher invited me to a Christian girls' camp during the school holidays. I had no idea how I was going to broach the subject with my dad. My mum had a word with him suggesting that it might be a good idea, as it would get me out of the house for a while. He relented. I was overjoyed. My teacher funded me, as we had no money for extras like that.

The time came for me to go; I was excited, as this was my first time away from home, but on arriving, I felt so ashamed that I was the only girl there with shabby clothes; I had no stories to tell about horse riding, tennis, swimming gala's or holidays like the other girls were sharing. I wanted to run and hide.

They obviously came from much better homes than I did. I was so insecure and shy I hardly spoke to a soul. I didn't know how to answer if someone came up and spoke to me, I wanted the ground to open up and swallow me.

In spite of that, I did enjoy the morning bible studies we had and the evening services. I had not heard about Christianity before. My parents were Roman Catholics, and the house was covered with various pictures of The Virgin Mary and Christ on the cross, but they never once attended church and their life was far from 'religious'. I then realised why my music teacher was so nice, she was a Christian. I heard about the love of God… this was a love I needed. An unconditional love. I learnt that had I been the only sinner in the world, Jesus would still have died for me. It has taken most of my life to really grasp that truth.

Whilst at that camp I received Jesus as my Lord and Saviour. I felt wonderful for the first time in my life. Surely now my life would change?

One unfortunate incident however caused me great confusion. Some of the older girls at camp were called 'officers' and it was their responsibility to check that the dormitories under their care were kept in a clean and tidy state.

The dormitory I was in was assigned to a girl we shall call Mary. One night after lights out, she came to the dormitory and asked me to go with her to her room as she had something she needed to discuss with me.

Being the timid person I, was I thought I had done something very wrong although I could not imagine what?

When we got to her room she sat me on the bed and proceeded to put her arms around me in a way that made me feel extremely uncomfortable. She then tried to kiss me. Just as she was about to do that the leader of the camp walked in… I was dispatched to my dormitory and told that I would be seen the next day.

That night seemed endless as I tossed and turned whilst sleep evaded me.

The next day I was called to see the camp head, only to be told that the officer had explained what happened. That I came to her room in a state of upset and she was trying to calm me down. I did not have the courage to challenge this. Once again, I felt the victim. Would this never end?

I would like to say that my life changed from that point but it didn't. I did however start praying for my parents, although if I'm truthful I still couldn't say that I loved my dad, or my uncle who had abused me.

I decided that I wanted to stay on at school and take my G.C.E.'s, as I wanted to go to the London Royal Academy of Music to study, and eventually hoped to become a music teacher.

However in the school holidays of my fourth year, my mother told me that I couldn't stay on at school as she only had six months to live, so she needed me to get a job and help support them.

My dream of the future I had planned for myself was shattered. Going to college would not only have given me the career of my dreams, but it would also have got me away from home, which is all I had been waiting for since the day I moved in.

I became a sales assistant in a tobacconist shop. The owner had just purchased it as his second shop. One morning I was in the basement stock room getting stock, when he crept up on me from behind and started fondling me. What was wrong with me that so many people felt they could abuse me? What signals was I giving out?

I was becoming quite desperate. I blamed myself and started getting suicidal thoughts -quite often.

If only I had known then what I know now about familiar spirits. These spirits can gain access into a person's life and the person need not be aware of it. As I was abused as a child whenever I was in a situation with a man I perceived as controlling, the 'it' in me summoned up familiar spirits in these men, leading them to try and take advantage of me causing my emotions to spiral out of control again.

One night on what had become the regular pub jaunt; my parents decided they wanted to stay until closing, so they asked the son of a friend of theirs to drive me home. I was fifteen. He was eighteen and he was looked on as the neighborhood stud - a handsome guy, desired by all the girls. All except me that was. He drove fast and went past my home out to a local park. By now, I was getting very scared. He consoled me by saying that I was different to all the other girls who usually threw themselves at him and he liked me. I confess to having felt quite pleased about what he had said. Upon entering the park, he asked if he could take me for a walk. My confidence was soaring.

When we were well away from the road, he started kissing me. I had never been kissed in the way he was kissing. Then it happened, he started ripping my clothes off. I do not know how I managed to escape, I ran to the bus stop only to see the last bus pulling away. I ran all the way home, which took about 20 minutes.

I arrived home panting and very red. My parents went into a rage, accusing me of all manner of things, calling me horrible names and ordering me to bed. I tried to explain what had just happened to me but they were in no mood to listen. I cried into my pillow asking God why my life was like this

Chapter 4

A New Man

Marriage should be honoured…
Hebrews chapter 13 verse 4

Having given my life to the Lord I wanted to start attending a church. My parents being non-practicing Roman Catholics said that if I needed to go to church then it should be a catholic one. I knew I needed more than that so I asked my music teacher what she recommended. She told me about her church and said I would be very welcome. I prayed before asking my parents, as I knew it would meet with resistance.

Eventually they agreed to my going, but I was only allowed to go to the evening service as Sunday morning was my 'chores' morning.

Nevertheless, I was delighted. In order to get to church I had to catch two buses. The journey took around 50 minutes. It was a large Baptist Church. I used to sit up in the balcony. There was a thriving youth group, but I never felt confident enough to sit with them or talk to them

I learnt so much by attending church. One of those being believers' baptism. I knew I had been christened as a baby, but how does a baby know what is happening? I learnt about Jesus going to John the Baptist in the desert and being baptised Himself. Scripture backed it up in Acts Chapter 2 verse 38 *"Repent and be baptised"* I knew then that this is something I had to do. I was fifteen years old and needed my parents' consent.

When I asked them if I could be baptised it was as if I had told them I was pregnant. My dad went crazy. After a few days and some persuasion from my mum, he finally relented. I was overjoyed. The evening came for my baptism and to my surprise; my mum came to see me.

It was an amazing experience and many times since, I have wished I could repeat it. It was witnessing this that my mum became a Christian.

Time passed and when I was sixteen, I was allowed into the pub. This remained a nightly visit for us. It was on one of those nights that I met a new young barman. He was nineteen almost twenty. We got talking and he told me he had a pop group called the 'Aliens' of all things. He said that he'd heard I was a singer, and asked me to be their vocalist.

Although I was shy and timid, I agreed, thinking that at least it would get me away from the house for a couple of hours.

The first night I went, I was introduced to the rest of the group. There was a guy on guitar, one on drums and a keyboard player. They asked if I could sing 'Hey Mr. Tambourine man'... I didn't even know it as I was so entrenched in classical music and never possessed a record player or radio. I told them I could sing 'Michael row the boat ashore! This was met with much hilarity, but Tom (the barman) defended me and so that's what we sang.

He walked me home that night and shook my hand asking if he could take me out one night. I was over the moon...me....small shy insignificant me being asked out.

Tom proved to be a perfect gentleman; he introduced me to his family, who were wonderful.

Although they lived on the same council estate as us, they were such a respectable family, so close. There were five other siblings and they all loved each other as well as their parents. I had never seen such a close family before.

When he continued to ask me out, I felt as if my life was finally changing. When he asked to marry me; I saw an escape from my awful situation. I did love him as much as I understood love at that age, and he appeared to be so kind and caring. I should have taken note of the warning signs though, as he had already hit me a few times when he was drunk. He was always so apologetic though, assuring me that he would never ever do it again. Unfortunately, that was not the case.

When we asked my parents for permission to be married, to say they were less than pleased would be an understatement. They agreed to us being engaged but told us clearly that we had to wait until I was twenty-one before we could marry. That was the age of consent in those days.

I was getting to the stage of not being able to cope much more with the constant violence, so I threatened my father with the news, that if he would not let us marry then I would get myself pregnant. I cannot begin to describe what happened after that! My father went into an almighty rage threatening to break every bone in my body. This was a favorite saying of his. My mother had to try to calm him down.

Months later, he eventually relented and agreed to us marrying. This we did when I was seventeen years old...

We found ourselves a dingy bedsit to live in. It was in a town house and we were on the first floor. There were eight other tenants of varying ages and we had to share a toilet and bathroom with them all! It was not what we would have chosen but it was all we could afford. At least I was away from all the violence.....or so I thought.

For a bride, part of the joy of getting married is the preparation stage. What sort of dress, how was I going to wear my hair, who was I going to choose as bridesmaids and so it goes on? I had none of this. My mother took over all the arrangements. She chose the dress and decided who the bridesmaids were going to be, she even chose what colour dresses they were going to wear.

I felt powerless, as I often did with her. She was a

strong, manipulative woman. She asked a friend of hers to be the photographer. On the wedding day, she took me off to another friend of hers to have my hair styled. I had long thick wavy hair, which fell beautifully around my shoulders. I often felt it was my best feature.

On arriving at her friend's house, she started to explain how she would like to see it styled. I ended up with a tomboy cut, similar to the style Mia Farrow used to wear, for those who remember her. It was almost a short back and sides. I was devastated. The headdress that my mother had chosen for me looked ridiculous with such short hair. I felt awful facing everyone when I arrived at the church.

The next fear I faced that day was how drunk my father would get. I was so worried about him ruining the whole day. By the time we were ready to leave for the church, he was indeed inebriated but at least he was not aggressive – yet.

The day passed in a haze. We had the service, and then went to a hall, which joined onto a pub! It just so happened that one of Tom's ex-girlfriends had arranged to be in the pub at that time and kept persuading him to dance. A fine wedding this was turning out to be.

That night we were driven back to our bedsit by my uncle of all people! We were spending the night there and the next morning were being driven, by my uncle again to a place in Sussex for our honeymoon. All this was arranged by my mother. She would not hear of the plans we had in wanting to go abroad.

On arrival, we found that our honeymoon accommodation was no more than a trailer caravan, in a field miles from anywhere. The only other caravan in the field was just packing up to go home as the season had finished.

There were no shops and only two buses a day. This meant we had to be up at the crack of dawn to catch the bus, which went to the railway Station. This was our only means of going anywhere. It was awful. We did not have the luxury of a car

Almost as soon as we married, Tom changed, becoming almost a carbon copy of my father! Drinking far too much and becoming physically violent towards me. What had I done? Why did my life have to be like this?

Chapter 5

Lost Children

With pain, you will give birth…
Genesis chapter 3 verse 16b

In the first three months of marriage, I suffered my first miscarriage. I had eight in all. Shortly after that, I conceived again. During this pregnancy, I was hospitalised several times as my body tried repeatedly to miscarry. This was mainly due to my husband being violent towards me. On one occasion he hit me so hard I fell to the floor. While I was lying there, Tom repeatedly kicked me in the stomach.

Shortly before my baby was due to be born one of the doctors warned us that there was a good chance my baby would be marked in some way, as they had to give me so many drugs to save me that they did not know what effect it would have on the baby.

The day came when I started labour, and a very frightened eighteen year old, who had no idea of what was about to happen went to the hospital. I had received no education as it were, on what happened during childbirth. Tom dropped me off and went home, or rather to the pub. I was alone and frightened. There was no internet back then, so I really had no idea on what I was about to face. I know it seems inconceivable now, but that's how it was.

In those days, you were ordered onto a hospital trolley and given an enema, then they placed a bedpan under you and there you sat. It was one of the most horrendous experiences I have ever had.

When I was taken into the labour room, making more than a little noise, I was told by a midwife that I was making too much fuss!

Sixteen hours later my son was born. I was unable to see him as he was rushed to the special care unit. Unlike today, information was not forth coming - after all I was only the mother so what did I know?

I was not to see my son until he was four days old. I was told that he was paralysed down the left side, and was having difficulty breathing. When Tom eventually returned to the hospital, he was shocked to see this little mite only able to move his right arm and leg; he also had a large red birthmark covering his forehead.

That day Tom cried out to God and pleaded with him to heal our child. If He did, then Tom vowed he would give his life to the Lord. Well my son was healed albeit he was in hospital for a couple of months. Tom, true to his word, committed his life to God. I thought that my dreams had come true. I was going to have the happy family life that had eluded me, as well as having a Christian husband supporting us. My children were going to be brought up in a wonderful happy family. How wrong could I have been.?

Tom turned out to be a Jekyll and Hyde Christian. His drinking continued, as did his violence. I had seven further miscarriages, each one broke my heart. They were all boys. Years later, I was able to joke about the fact that had they all lived I would have had a football team!

I then had another live son and almost three years after him I had a stillborn son.

Following his traumatic birth I had to have an emergency hysterectomy…I was one month away from my twenty third birthday!

Having been in labour for three days the registrar decided to call in the consultant for permission to do a caesarian. It was late in the evening by the time he arrived. He was dressed up in a dinner suit and smelt of alcohol. He thought I was too young to be scarred, as in those days they didn't practice the bikini type surgery. He told the registrar to put up a drip in order to make the contractions stronger.

On the third day, I started to give birth. We knew something was not quite right when the nurse went out of the room and came back with another fetal heart-monitoring machine. She told us the first one was broken. A few moments after this everything went crazy. Doctors and nurses rushed into the room from all directions. The headboard was ripped off my bed and the bed was turned around.

I had no idea what was happening, nobody bothered to explain anything to me. They told Tom that he had to leave. I started to give birth. Having a baby is supposed to be a joyous occasion but this was like being in the middle of a nightmare.

Sometime later, I felt my baby emerge and saw the doctor lay him next to me on a table. They were working on him and I was watching. Still nobody bothered to explain what was happening. I remember asking repeatedly if everything was all right but my questions were ignored.

After what seemed like an eternity, my baby was wrapped up and taken away. I asked if they were taking him to the special care baby unit, as I had experienced this with my first son so I knew the drill. It was then that the doctor came and stood by my bed and told me that my son was dead. Apparently, the placenta had broken away.

Everything in the room started going around and around. I was dreaming surely. This couldn't be happening. I had carried him for nine months and now I wasn't even allowed to see him let alone hold him. I was asked if I had a name for him. It was Paul Daniel. My son…

Following the birth, the hospital almoner visited me, which is like a social worker today. She asked what arrangements I had for the disposal of my son. Nothing like this had ever happened to me before, how was I supposed to know what happened in times like this? I asked her what the hospital could arrange and I was told that the only thing they would do would be to use the incinerator! I went hysterical. This was my son she was talking about.

A week later, I was discharged. We set about making our own funeral arrangements for our little boy. It was to be a little white coffin and he was to be buried, as I couldn't bear the thought of cremation after this callous woman's comment.

The day before the funeral, I was rushed back into hospital hemorrhaging. The doctor had a word with Tom to explain that as they were not sure what was causing it, they would like to operate. They explained that if they found any damage to the uterus they would try to repair it. Tom told them not to do that, he would rather they remove it altogether.

Following the surgery I was seriously ill and put in the Intensive Therapy Unit where my husband was given the guest room next door, as they didn't expect me to survive. I had lost an inordinate amount of blood and had a nasty infection. I also developed peritonitis and my right lung had virtually given up. My mother came to visit me once, as she said she couldn't cope with seeing all the tubes that were going in to my body, so I never saw her again while I was in ITU.

During my time there, I had an experience I shall never forget. One day when experiencing particularly bad pain, I was lifted out of my body and was actually looking down on it. All the pain had left me and everything around me was bright light and so peaceful. It was an amazing sensation. I saw doctors and nurses surround my bed busying themselves with all manner of things, which I could not make out.

I remember saying out loud, "I can't leave, I have two little boys who need me" After what seemed an eternity, I became aware of intense pain once more and found that I was back.

I was in ITU for almost two weeks before I was deemed well enough to return to a normal ward. The actual ward they put me on was the Postnatal ward! Thankfully, I did have a side room to myself.

Each night I would lay awake hearing the babies crying, longing for one of them to be mine. I knew God had His hands on me and was so comforted by that. What was not very comforting were the Christian friends who visited me, asking what sin I had committed to go through all this. I knew at that point just how Job in the Old Testament must have felt. I knew where the saying 'Jobs Comforters' came from.

I remained in hospital for three months, during which time I applied to adopt a baby girl. If this had happened today, my application would be thrown out straight away. I was still grieving; it would be seen as a replacement child and so on.

Miraculously my application was accepted and the wheels were put in motion. There was no counseling offered to me for either giving birth to a stillborn son or applying for adoption! Even as I write this, I find it inconceivable that I was treated in such a way. It would not happen in the days we now live in.

I was eventually discharged from hospital, still very weak and vulnerable. The adoption process carried on and the following January we went to collect our 'daughter'. She was eleven months old, and six weeks younger than my son would have been. She had been fostered from birth but the foster mother had so many other children that she was finding it difficult to cope with them all.

During this year of waiting, I had to undergo nine more operations due to complications arising from the traumatic birth and the hysterectomy. Following one of them, I developed an abscess on my scar, which became infected. The nurse used to visit each day once I returned home. When my husband saw it, he held me in front of our full-length mirror exposing the scar and told me that he found me repulsive. I cannot begin to tell you how that made me feel. Why didn't I die on the operating table? How much longer was I going to be treated in this way?

That night we went to bed as usual and upon waking in the morning, I found that he had gone. He had left me and I had no idea where he was. He did not even leave a note. I only knew that I was weak, emotional and had two little boys and a little girl to look after.

I had to explain to his employers that he had gone away. This posed its own problems as we lived in tied accommodation.

I later discovered that he had gone to stay several miles away with one of the doctors who had operated on me with whom we had become close friends.

I had a call from the doctor the next night informing me that he had persuaded Tom to return home to me. I felt like changing the locks, but knew that whatever he had done to me God still loved him and he was still my husband.

Coupled with that my children were missing him, I was determined that they would never know what their father was really like.

Chapter 6

An Old Love

Place me like a seal over your heart...
Song of Songs chapter 8 verse 6

The years passed - although sometimes I thought they never would. I had to go out to work as we were extremely poor. There were times when I was afraid to come home, as I did not know what awaited me. Tom was drinking quite heavily again. He had also started heavy flirting with friends of mine, which left me feeling embarrassed and ugly. He was slowly destroying me.

It was during this time that a friend of Tom's from our church, who himself had suffered a great deal physically started showing me the first bit of compassion I had known. I longed to have a husband like that. Inevitably, we became attracted to each other and became very close. It is only by the grace of God that we never actually consummated our relationship.

One day I received a letter from a friend to say that she had noticed that my friendship with Colin was becoming too close, and suggested I do something about it before Tom found out. I was incensed. How dare people judge me when they had no idea of the nightmare I was living?

Our relationship continued and we enjoyed each other's company. I actually laughed when I was with Colin. I enjoyed the feeling of someone actually caring for me. I used to fantasise about what would happen if anything happened to Tom. I could marry the man who had become a lifeline to me.

Several months passed until one day my world was rocked, yet again.

I met Colin for coffee in a cosy little café and he told me that we had to stop all this. People were beginning to notice and he had a reputation in the church. I wanted to run out and throw myself under the first bus that came along. How could I survive without him? Our relationship was not even sexual; it had gone deeper than that. I loved him and he had told me that he loved me also. What was I going to do?

The days following that final meeting were endless and black. I did all the things I had to do, cooking, cleaning, taking and collecting the children to and from school but it was as if I was in automatic. I was empty, devoid of all feeling.

Eventually months passed, and I suppose the pain diminished. It was not made easier by the fact that Colin still featured very heavily in Tom's life, which meant that I also had to keep seeing him.

Around this time, Tom decided that as I no longer had a uterus, it gave him a sexual freedom he had not experienced before. He became addicted to sex, virtually raping me several times a day. It was at this time that I really did want to die. It became obvious to me that my life was never going to improve.

I tried taking pills in front of Tom in the hope it might show him how desperate I was but all he did was hit me, laugh and go to the pub.

Several weeks later when Tom was at work he injured his back. He had a slipped disc, which meant he had to be on his back for weeks on end. When that didn't work, he had to wear a plaster cast from under his arms to the bottom of his stomach. This created some laughter in the home as people came to sign it. For a time things seemed to get better. Nothing was permanent though. Life continued to be the roller coaster ride I had come to hate. Maybe that's why I hate roller coasters to this day.

The plaster never worked, so he had to have surgery. This was an amazing time. I had to drive sixty miles every day to visit him as well as care for the children, yet I felt safe for the first time in my life. I could make decisions regarding the children, I could decide what they could and could not eat, and when they were tucked up in bed I could sit and for the first time relax truly relax. It was a wonderful feeling.

When Tom was discharged from hospital, it was decided that he could no longer do the job he had been doing. Now he was unemployed and the usual routine commenced once again. When he was in a good mood, he was amazing. Very funny and good to be with, but when the mood changed it was horrible.

Fortunately, I needed to go out to work again, as there was no way we could manage on the benefits Tom was getting. This was an escape for me for a few hours.

We were living in tied accommodation, which we were now going to have to leave. It was the best house I had ever had and now we were going to lose it. Shortly after this, the council re-housed us. We were given a three bed roomed house on a small estate. It could have been worse, but there was no choice given, we were just 'put' there!

Money was so very tight. I remember one day having nothing at all in the cupboards. My children would not be able to have breakfast let alone packed lunch. That night I prayed with them that Jesus would provide. We made it a policy that we never told anybody from our church about the severity of our situation because it was amazing just watching how the Lord provided.

The next morning there was a box on our doorstep, which was full up with food. Even chocolate bars for the children, which was a rare treat for them.

Years passed and I was growing increasingly unhappy. My husband put his love of football before anything else. Many times, we had arranged for friends to visit in the evening, but on discovering there was a football match on TV, he made me phone them to cancel, giving some lame excuse.

Year followed year and I grew increasingly unhappy. One Sunday we went to church as usual but on returning home my husband suffered a heart attack. He was rushed to hospital. Naturally the children were distraught.

When the coronary care unit carried out their tests, they found that he had a rare heart disease that was probably congenital.

He was in and out of hospital for the next three years. During this time, he became addicted to the pain medication he had to take. It was a morphine derivative. When the doctors tried to wean him off he became more aggressive than I had seen him in a long time.

He could no longer work and became more dominant than ever. He continued as a Jekyll & Hyde Christian. By this I mean that when he was 'up' it was amazing, he would study his bible for hours and was committed to our fellowship, wanting to be at all the various meetings and social activities, but when he was down he started drinking again and although he was not so physically violent he 'nagged' which I found so much worse.

As a result of the stress I was under, I was referred to a cardiologist due to some problems I was experiencing. I had an erratic heartbeat and pains in the chest. I could not live like this much longer.

Chapter 7

A New Way

Do you not know that the wicked will not inherit…
1 Corinthians chapter 6 verse 9

Each time Tom went into hospital he was nursed by an amazing ward sister who went to a church along the coast from where we lived. She was so kind and understanding to both of us.

On one occasion when he was in hospital, she came to visit to see if I was all right. I discovered that I enjoyed her visit so much that I could not wait for her to come again.

She started visiting on a regular basis and before I knew what was happening we had drifted into a relationship. I suppose it would be called a lesbian relationship although I never saw myself as a lesbian. All I knew was that for the first time in my life I had found somebody who truly cared for me. She treated me like a person, with feelings, choices and opinions, and we had fun together.

She didn't try to control me.

I was becoming increasingly uncomfortable at church, and could not take communion. I knew what I was doing was wrong but seemed powerless to do anything about it. Maybe the truth was I chose not to do anything about it.

One day when I returned from work Tom started on at me again and something snapped inside me. I told him I was leaving to go to live with Annabel. He told me that there was no way I could take my children, and he made me tell them that I could no longer stay with them.

That was the darkest moment of my life, but I just couldn't stay any longer. I left that night and moved in with Annabel. I was nursing at that time so was financially independent.

The next night the elders of the church visited us. They tried their best to make me aware of what I was doing but I had started on a slippery slope down and ignored their pleas. One thing I did feel uncomfortable about though was the title I was being given. Lesbians! I could not accept that. I was probably being extremely naïve but everywhere we went I introduced her as my sister. It was the most amazing mixture of emotions. On the one hand feeling loved for the first time in my life, grieving for my children and also the happy family life I had always longed for and feeling such shame that I was living with a woman!

I was not allowed to have my children visit me in my new home. When I saw them, it had to be on neutral territory. Therefore, in mid-winter we met in a cold wimpy bar. I loathed what I was doing but for the first time in my life, I felt like a person in my own right. I had someone who cared for me and treated me well. I could put my key in the lock without that deep fear in the pit of my stomach that had become part of my life, wondering what I was going to face on the other side.

This began my fifteen years away from the Lord. In spite of having more money than I had ever had, travelling to wonderful places abroad – a thing I had never done before – and not living in constant fear, deep down inside, I was unhappy.

I missed my children desperately; I hated myself for what I was doing. The pull to come back to the Lord was so strong but I equated coming back with having to live the life I was forced to live before…and there was no way I could face that.

When the initial shock had worn off, Tom and I became closer than when we lived together. I supported him financially paying many of his bills. Anything concerned with the children we decided together. If only we could have been like this when we were married. Sadly we were now divorced.

Six years after I moved out, the unimaginable happened and Tom died. This threw me into another spiral. I lived with so much guilt as it was. How could I cope with anymore?

My daughter who was now sixteen years old came to live with us. She started Sixth Form College and things seemed to be leveling out.

Four years later, Annabel had a major mental breakdown. She was hospitalised for several weeks. When she was discharged, it was agreed that we would move house in order to be nearer to my family as we were quite isolated where we lived. I nursed her for five years.

This was no easy task as she was quite depressed and used to sit in her chair stabbing herself with a fork. My children were now grown up and although I did not deserve it, they still loved me.

One of my sons lived close by and supported me enormously.

As her breakdown was a direct result of bullying at work, I enlisted the services of a solicitor in order to sue the company. This dragged on for years but in the end, she received a lump sum from them as an out of court settlement. We decided to put it towards purchasing a house as the one we had been living in was rented,

We found a house that needed a lot of work done on it to bring it up to the twentieth century. This was going to be fun after all the years of trying to fight a large company.

Once we had moved in and put our stamp on the house, she broke the news to me that whilst in hospital she had met another woman. While I was out at work trying to support us, this other woman had been visiting her. I was devastated.

She said she was moving out to be with her new partner. Once again, I wanted to die. What was I to do? I could not manage to pay a mortgage and all the household bills on my salary. Fortunately, Annabel continued to help financially until I could make other arrangements.

After she left, I could eat nothing for a whole month I lost three stone during that time. We had been together for 15 years. I could not believe this was happening.

I felt as if I had lost everything in my life. My children were grown up and I had nothing to live for. I even did a video tape saying my farewells to them.

Chapter 8

A New Life

Ask and it will be given to you, seek and you will find, knock and the door will be opened to you...
Matthew chapter 7 verse 7

THEN GOD...

I have to say that for the 15 years I was away from the Lord, the 'pull' on me to return was so strong. The stronger it got the lower I deliberately went, thinking that it would stop. I am so very grateful that God never gives up.

One day I had an overwhelming urge to return to church. Could I be forgiven for all that I had done? I looked up the names of churches that were local to me, and found one that met in a local school. I felt this would be the one that had what I was looking for. One that worshipped freely without the religiosity that so many churches had.

I went along to the school one Sunday and waited,

as there was no one there, and waited... and waited. Nobody showed up. I took this to mean that God did not want me back at all and returned home. As the week went on I realised that I had been silly and there was probably a very good explanation as to why nobody turned up. A weekend away together perhaps?

Therefore, the next Sunday I went along again, nothing! Nobody! Back home again. By now, I was convinced that God really did not want me. I talked with my daughter to explain what had happened. She looked up the church in her copy of the church directory and found the name of the leader. She was not giving up even if I was. She gave me his phone number.

I spent the week deliberating as to whether I should phone or not. Finally, late Saturday night I decided I had nothing to lose, so I phoned. I was answered by a lovely sounding woman who explained that they no longer met in that school, but had moved to another one in the area. She said she would look out for me the next day. So now, I was committed to going as she had taken my phone number.

I went along and was given the most amazing welcome from the loveliest people. The service was free and informal. I felt as if I had come home!

On returning to my house, I flung myself onto my knees, confessed everything of the past fifteen years to the Lord, reveled in His forgiveness and asked for a fresh infilling of His Holy Spirit.

I was surrounded with warmth and what I can only describe as a blanket of love. I wept before Him for ages. For the first time in my life, I wanted God so much that it hurt.

I continued going to all the meetings that were available. I was hungry for all I could get of God. I had so many years to make up for. After going along for a few weeks I was informed that the church was attending a Christian Retreat Centre for an away day. A day of fellowship and bible teaching. I was asked if I could give a lift to one of the lady's from church. I readily agreed.

This was my first challenge. I was painfully shy, and although I had been attending church on my own, I was in control as to who I spoke with or not as the case may be. I could never think of what to say to people. I knew, though, that I had to offer a lift to this lady.

One beautiful sunny Saturday, having mustered all my courage I went to collect Kathy. I was so nervous as to what we were going to talk about on the 30-minute journey; I was practicing to myself on the way to her house!

I need not have worried. On the journey, Kathy who incidentally had about 12 cats – dominated the conversation, which suited me fine. On arriving at the place, we went in to the coffee area.

That was when it happened… I saw a man walking across the far side of the room. A man I had not seen before at church. It was then that I understood how God could put words into a person's mouth! I found myself saying to Kathy "Who is that man"? She told me that was 'their John', no sooner had she said that, I said, "Is he married"? What! Where did that come from? I wanted to hide in the nearest cupboard! I could not believe what had just come out of my mouth!
Kathy told me that he was divorced and was raising his two boys on his own. For the rest of that day my mind was in a whirl. What had happened back there?

After the first session, we broke for lunch. If anyone had asked me what the session was about; I do not think I would have been able to tell them. I remember I sat on one of the round dining tables with about seven others. There was a man called Alan next to me who didn't stop talking about all the things he had achieved in his career in the theatre. I was glad that I didn't have to think of anything to say.

After lunch, we went back into the conference room and I became aware of John coming over towards me. We exchanged a brief conversation and then the session started. I don't remember much more of that day, except I remember feeling very glad to get home. Not because I hadn't enjoyed the day, but I was still reeling from the earlier incident.

Five months past and I saw John most weeks at church. We would exchange pleasantries after service whilst having coffee. He was a really nice man. Gentle, understanding and nothing like the men I had known or who been part of my life previously. He showed me that actually there were nice men out there after all.

People say that things are more obvious to 'outsiders' than to the people concerned. John and I experienced that. We were asked if we would be happy to be welcomers on the door at church.

How strange that we should be placed together! I approached the first week of welcoming duty with trepidation. What would I say to the people coming in let alone having to talk with John?

Our first week arrived and I found out so much about him during that time together. One thing I found amazing was that he was exactly nine months older than I was. This became quite precious to us as time went on. You see when he was born I was conceived. God planned us as soul mates right from the beginning.

It wasn't long before I found myself being drawn to John. I missed him when he wasn't around. What was happening? I did not want another relationship – ever! However hard I tried I could not get him out of my thoughts. When I returned from work, I found myself wondering what he was doing. Would he be thinking of me in the same way?

One Sunday I decided that I had to know if the same emotions were plaguing him. After the service when we were having coffee, I mentioned that I had quite a bad leak coming from my overflow water pipe. I knew that he was an avid DIY. expert so was convinced he would offer to help. He said he would see what he could do. I was strangely excited at the prospect of seeing him during the week.

The following Sunday arrived and I still had my leak! John approached me after the service apologetically explaining that he had been busy during the week. I fully understood and expected him to say he would visit during the following week.

Imagine the emotions that coursed through me when he gave me a card advertising a plumber! I was devastated.

On returning home, I tried to calm myself down. I also determined to stop thinking about John, as it was obvious his feelings were not the same. Try as I might though, the thoughts of him would not go away.

The following week I thought I would make myself vulnerable once more. I told John that I was going to the movies to see 'The Prince of Egypt'. This was an animated story of Moses, which had excellent reviews. I asked if he would like to come along. Initially he agreed and I was delighted, but a few minutes later, he said he had forgotten that he had an appointment and could not come.

That was it as far as I was concerned! I had been rejected twice now. Didn't he realise just what it had cost me to ask him? I have always been so shy; I even surprised myself at my boldness.

I now knew that I had to continue with the rest of my life on my own and stop all the silly girlie nonsense. Mmmnn, this was easier said than done! My mind was in torment. I just could not stop thinking about him. Every time we spoke at church, I discovered more and more that here was one of the nicest men I had ever met. So compassionate and funny, it did not seem fair that all these wonderful qualities were encased in one man.

As Christmas approached, I knew what I had to do to finally stop this torture in my mind. I was visiting my son for Christmas Day, which fell on a Saturday. On the three hour drive to him, I laid a fleece before the Lord. I said that if, when John and I met the following day at church, he didn't ask me out then I would know for sure that we were not meant to be together and I would finally stop all this nonsense. However if we were meant to be together, then before we parted he would ask me out. That would do it. Christmas day was torture. All the family were together having a wonderful time, but all I could think about was what would happen the following day. This decision was going to affect the rest of my life!

Chapter 9

A New Union

I will restore back to you the years the locusts have eaten…
Joel chapter 2 verse 25

When I got to church the following day, John was already there. This was unusual for him because he was usually on the late side.

We got talking and the subject of New Year's Eve came up, so I asked him what he was doing. He told me that he had been invited to a party, but he didn't want to go as he thought it would be boring. Just then the service was about to start so I went to my seat, which was a couple of rows away from him.

I immediately spoke with the Lord and asked him to forget what I had prayed the previous day. No way did I want a 'party pooper' for a partner!

After the service, we went to the kitchen as usual for tea and coffee. John was being spoken to by several other people. It came time for me to leave so I went over to him to say good-bye. I said that whatever he did decide to do on New Year's Eve I hoped he had a good time. I then started down the corridor, which led out to the playground where our cars were parked.

Suddenly I heard footsteps behind me. I took a quick glance and saw that it was John. At that point, I thought my heart was going to leave my chest! Just then, someone who needed to speak with him called him back. It seemed that any plans he had to speak further with me were thwarted.

I reached the car and had my hand on the door handle when I heard a voice….."What are you doing then on New Year's Eve?" I said that I was going to have a glass of wine and a mince pie and probably settle down in front of the television, to which the reply came…."do you want to go out then?"

I tell you it was like something out of Romeo and Juliet…!

My reply was just as casual though… "might as well, better than being stuck in alone!"

John said he would phone me to make arrangements. When I drove off my heart was racing, my knees were weak and I felt elated. A fine reaction from someone who never wanted to entertain the thought of another relationship.

Sunday to Friday seemed an eternity. My sister was a hairdresser and was as excited as I was when I told her that I wanted a hairstyle to remember. It was wonderful now to be in a close relationship with the sister who for so many years had hated me.

We had remained distant; hardly speaking with each other until four years previously, we both realised that it was actually our mother who had tried to keep us apart. We determined then to get to know each other. We found that we were alike in so many ways and started to enjoy each other's company.

I told my work colleagues that I had a date on New Year's Eve. Some were delighted and some rather bemused.

Eventually Friday arrived. John had arranged to collect me at 7pm. I was so nervous it was bordering on the ridiculous. He duly arrived and off we went to the party. He was quite right though - it was boring and we left around 11pm. On arriving home, I felt it only polite to invite him in for coffee, which he accepted.

We talked and talked. It was as if we had known each other all our lives. I found myself telling him about all the babies I had lost, and he was so understanding. I hadn't meant to go into all that but he seemed to draw it out of me.

We were sitting on opposites sides of my lounge. As midnight approached, I left my chair and went over to join him on the settee. When the clock struck twelve, I wished John a happy new year and gave him a quick hug.

By 12:06, we had become an item. There would be no going back now. God had shown what he wanted for us and that was to be together. One of the first verses He gave us was that He was going to restore the years the locusts had eaten.

 We planned our wedding for October but married in May in a registry office. It was expensive to run both our homes and we found that we just wanted to be together after all we were not spring chickens. However, we continued with our plans for a big church wedding in October.

My sister had a friend who made wedding dresses so we had great fun planning together what I was going to wear. This was a special time for me for two reasons. Firstly, it was great fun planning my wedding as my first one had been completely taken over by my mother.

Secondly, my sister and I had only become close over the previous four years. As we were not raised together, we had no bonding as it were. Coupled with that, when my sister was married and children started coming along our attempts to get to know each other were sabotaged by my mother who couldn't stand us being together.

She did everything in her power to keep us apart. It was as if she was jealous of any relationship we were trying to make with each other.

Fortunately, we did become close and we shared a great time in planning my wedding.

Sadly, though in the months leading up to it, my sister was diagnosed with cancer. She had been misdiagnosed by her doctor, so by the time they found it, it had gone too far.

Eleven days before my wedding while she was on a weekend leave from hospital, she phoned me to say the silk bouquet she was making for me was almost finished. We also spoke about how we would decorate her wheelchair with ribbons and balloons. My sister was a real party animal. I told her that I would dance her wheelchair around the dance floor all night.

We had that conversation on a Sunday evening. Monday morning my nephew telephoned me with the news that my sister had died in the early hours. I will never forget the emotions that ran through my body. Anger, grief and an immense feeling of loss were but a few.

I couldn't believe it. John and I drove the hour's journey to the hospital, I needed to see her. That is the only way I would believe that she really had gone.

We entered her room and saw her there in the bed. She was unrecognisable. This didn't seem fair. I had only had a sister for four years and now she was gone. This was supposed to be one of the happiest weeks for me, and now this.

The funeral was held four days before the wedding. My niece did an amazing job of organizing the day to reflect my sister's character. After the funeral, we went back to her house to find it full of helium balloons. They were everywhere. I suppose some people might have thought it irreverent, but for those who knew my sister, it was just what she would have wanted.

When the wedding day arrived, I knew that I had to carry on as if she were there. The church service was wonderful. It was filled with family and so many friends, it was full to capacity.

We had a wonderful reception. The atmosphere was electric. Everybody ate, drank and danced the night away. It was a perfect day in every way. A Jaguar car arrived to whisk us away to the airport for our honeymoon.

I would like to say that we lived happily ever after, but our first year together was awful. We had both been on our own for such a long time, we had become very independent and adjusting to another person in the home was so very hard for us both.

I also discovered at this time that the abuse I had suffered from my father, as well as my first husband had made me ultra-sensitive to any change in

John's tone of voice, body language or general atmosphere.

I became so tense inside if any or all of these things occurred. I needed to know immediately if I had done or said something wrong. It was a horrible place to live from. As the years went on and healing came, the sensitivity stayed with me, but now instead of the feelings of fear, I found I was able to discern things in many people, which has been invaluable.

God kept us together during those painful months. Several times, I went to leave but remembered the fleece I had put before the Lord and how he had answered it. Deep down I knew we had a wonderful future together, however hard it seemed at the time.

Time passed by and we had to move to another county for John's work. We set about finding a church. One Sunday we attended a New Frontiers Church, which I knew John would probably not want to settle in, as he did not really like New Frontiers. To my surprise, he loved it saying that this was the place he felt we should be. Surprisingly I was the one who objected. I spent years in a New Frontiers Church and loved it, so was quite confused by my feelings over this one.

John agreed that we could try another fellowship the following week. We went to an Assemblies of God. I liked it and asked if we could settle there. John agreed. We spent six months there until some things occurred that we were not comfortable with. John suggested we return to the New Frontiers International Church.

The first Sunday back there, they had an altar call at the end. I told John that I felt I had to go forward even though I didn't understand why. He came to support me. A lovely married couple came up to pray with me. As soon as they started praying, I started sobbing uncontrollably. So much so that they took me to the back of the church. They tried to find out why I was in the state I was in.

After several minutes, it all came tumbling out about my abusive uncle. They said that this needed ministry and agreed to visit us during the week. We lived in a tiny first floor flat, which was tied accommodation. I was quite nervous about inviting anybody there as I guess I felt ashamed of it. They were lovely though and soon put us at ease. It was a painful few weeks of ministry because once I had started telling them about my past, everything came out.

After a few weeks of their ministering to me on a weekly basis, I felt freer than I had in many years. It was wonderful. I then understood why it was that the first week we had visited the church I was the one who didn't want to stay there. The enemy loves to keep people in chains. I no longer had those chains around my ankles. I was free!

Fifteen months passed and I had to travel about 350 miles round trip from where we were living on a weekly basis to visit our parents, as both John's father and my mother were becoming increasingly frail. One day both John and I were led to the verse from   Exodus Chapter 20 verse 12 *Honor your father and mother...*

We both felt that we needed to move back down south in order to care for them. This saddened us as we had made many friends in the area we lived. We had also found a 'home' in the fellowship we belonged to. We couldn't think about moving unless a job came up for John. Therefore, we waited.

In only a matter of weeks, John's company advertised for a manager in a town, which was only about twenty minutes' drive from our parents' town. John applied and not surprisingly, he was given the job. The Lord had gone before us once again. We said our sad farewells and departed for the next chapter of our lives

Having moved to yet another tied property, which was only marginally bigger than the last one, we went about finding a fellowship, but we could never quite get settled. The lounge was so small we could never have friends around for a meal, as there was nowhere to put them. I started to become very frustrated with the place. We knew we could never afford our own property, and felt secure in the knowledge that on retirement we would be provided with accommodation from the council. We still couldn't understand why we were finding it so hard to settle in our local fellowship.

After church one Sunday, I sensed the Lord was asking me to be content with where I was and with what I had. I struggled with this a little but eventually from the bottom of my heart, I told the Lord that I truly was content, and if He intended that, we should stay here for the remainder of our working lives then that was all right by me.

The following week having spent two years there, John went to a company meeting to be told that in the not too distant future all residential managers' jobs would be going. When the question was raised about alternative accommodation, they were told they needed to make their own arrangements!

We were distraught by this news. There was no way we could save, as John's salary was so low we couldn't even pay all the bills on his income. I had to work, as well. It was at this time that I had two nasty car crashes within a year of each other. Neither one was my fault. In the second one, I sustained fractured ribs and a cracked sternum as well as whiplash.

If the council did house us, we faced being put on an awful estate in the middle of town. I was becoming frantic with worry, but eventually handed it over to the Lord.

Chapter 10

A New Home

God has planned something better for us...
Hebrews chapter 11 verse 40

One week later, we went to London for a family get together. We met my two sons and daughter, along with the grandchildren in Covent Garden. It was a beautifully hot sunny day and the atmosphere was electric. Stalls laden with all manner of colorful materials. The smell of coffee and food wafting up from the eateries down below. Street performers amazing all the children with their tricks. It was perfect.

We found a lovely place to have lunch together. We all sat under the largest canopy I have ever seen. The ambiance was wonderful, sitting outside protected from the sun by the canopy and enjoying all the aromas and sounds that were invading our senses.

After lunch, we moved onto another part of

Covent Garden where we found a delightful wine bar. Once again, we sat in the courtyard enjoying the summer day. We had just taken our first sip of wine, when my youngest son told us that we should start visiting estate agents when we return home. When we asked why, he told us that he was buying us a house!

I cannot begin to explain what emotions were coursing through my body. Only the week before I had arrived at that place of contentment with what we had, and now we had not only been told that we were being brought a house but that we had free choice as to where it would be. We went home on cloud nine.

In the ensuing weeks, we started to pray about where this house should be. We felt the Lord was taking us back to the town where we had first met. Once again, the Lord was going before us and John was offered a job as a deputy manager with Mencap. He was more than a little unsure, as he had never worked with the learning disabled before.

We found a lovely house and started all the preparations for moving. Coupled with this John had started his training for his new position. As we lived in tied accommodation, we had to vacate that, so for a short time we were technically homeless. Fortunately, my eldest son had recently moved leaving two months lease on the flat he had been renting. Armed with a blow up airbed and a garden bistro table and two chairs we stayed in this empty flat.

John studied hard as there was an awful lot to get through. He found that as he did so, he become increasingly interested in the aims and objects of his new role. However, on the day he was due to start his first shift, I was rushed from work into hospital with severe chest pains.

John had to call his new manager to explain. Not a good start to his new career. I was kept in hospital for monitoring. They started a regime of blood thinning medication. Praise God it was nothing serious.

Eventually the day came for the move and we were as excited as children. It did not take us long to settle into our new home. If we thought our life was going to settle into a nice quiet routine, once again we were mistaken.

John had to take his residents away for their annual holiday. The residents decided they would like a long boat holiday, so it was duly booked.

Around that time, the country had experienced severe floods and we were not sure if the holiday would still be on. A couple of days before John was due to go he checked with the boating company only to be told that everything was running normally.

John had never piloted a boat before and on arriving on the Avon and Kennet Canal found that the long boat he was expecting was actually a barge type boat. Never one to be daunted John set about getting all the residents on board and away they went.

Within a very short time, they were in difficulty. The water was running so fast the barge was being thrown all over the place. John kept going, doing the best he could. He was drinking a copious amount of water as the stress of it was making his mouth extremely dry. A few hours later, he began to feel decidedly ill.

The following day he could do very little. On the third day, they had to send for help. The conditions were proving very unsafe and John was growing weaker and weaker.

When the person arrived to help them back, he noticed a strange colour to the drinking water and investigated. It transpired that the person responsible for filling the water containers on the boat before renting it out had inadvertently put toilet water in the drinking water and visa versa!

John had been poisoned with formaldehyde. He was taken to the local hospital once they had been safely brought back to the boat yard.

Fortunately, he had the presence of mind to take a sample of the water and passed it on to the local environmental health officer.

When he eventually arrived back home, he was an emotional wreck. He needed three months off work to recover. Various people in the medical profession advised us that formaldehyde is a carcinogenic and they were uncertain how this could affect him in the future.

We knew that God has a plan for our lives and nothing or nobody can thwart that. We were secure in the Lord.

Time passed and we settled into our fellowship. We became home group leaders and general all round host and hostess, as we loved doing barbeques for the fellowship. Life was good. We thought that the worst years were now behind us.

In 2007, John's dad had a nasty fall and broke his hip. This concerned us greatly as we knew that in a person of his age the prognosis was never very good. Several years before this happened he was living quite happily and independently in his bungalow. We lived just around the corner and called in most days to check on him. We always enjoyed our time with him, as he was so cheerful all the time. He was a wonderful man. Many times, we would visit him and noted how his joints were swollen with arthritis, it was obvious that he was in pain, yet he never complained. He was always cheerful and a joy to visit.

He was the sort of father I would have loved. John had many stories and memories from his childhood about happy Christmases and birthdays he had been given by his parents.

One spring day we visited him as usual and were told by dad that John's sister was going to be moving in with him. He said this was not what he wanted as he enjoyed living on his own. We suggested that he tell her this, but he didn't feel able to. He asked if John would advocate for him. John readily agreed.

A family meeting was called, which included John's brother and sister in law, his sister and brother in law and us. Before we arrived at the meeting, they had already 'persuaded' dad that it really was the best thing if they moved in. Dad was old and no longer had the capacity to stand his ground, so he capitulated.

That was the beginning of the end for him. He no longer had to make his own lunchtime sandwich, which incidentally he enjoyed doing. He never had to think about what he was going to eat, so slowly but surely, he started to decline in health.

By the time he broke his hip in 2007 he didn't have much strength left to fight for recovery. He died later that year. He left a huge gap in our lives. Dad was the nearest person to a loving parent I had ever had, apart from my aunty.

He left a will stating that his property had to be sold and divided three ways. This was when the problems started. It was obvious that John's sister and brother in law did not intend to move out!

They even asked both John and his brother if they would forgo their portion of the inheritance until they died, so they could continue to live in the bungalow. When they were told it had to be sold they started looking for property of the same value, even though both John and his brother were not willing to let them have their share.

John works in the housing field and offered them so much advice, which they refused to take. Unfortunately it began to turn nasty. We had to enlist the services of a solicitor. That didn't put them off though. They fought tooth and nail. This stress lasted for two years until finally they moved out.

While all this was happening my son suggested that we put our home on the market, which was his after all, and he would buy the bungalow. It was not going to be easy to sell, as they had made it virtually unlivable.

We took his advice and put our house on the market. It didn't take long to sell, and the arrangements were made to move into the bungalow. On the move day, my daughter came around with me to clean up before the furniture arrived. We walked into the hallway and were met with the filthiest place we have ever seen.

In the weeks and months that followed, we had to strip everything out. Carpets, wallpaper, bath, toilets and old furniture that had been left there. It was a mammoth task and there were days when I wondered if we would ever get things straight.

Eventually everything was done. The bungalow looked like a different place. The Lord was so good because when John's sister was living in the bungalow, thinking that they would be there ad infinitum, they spent dad's money in having a completely new kitchen installed, new soffits and fascias, complete loft insulation as well as cavity walling.

The two years of legal wrangling had taken its toll. We were emotionally drained. However, all that was behind us now and we could settle into our new life in our wonderful, now clean and fresh bungalow

Chapter 11

A New Career

There is now NO condemnation for those who are in Christ Jesus...
Romans chapter 8 verse 1

As I retired in the summer of 2010, we decided that we would take the holiday of a lifetime and go to California on a coach tour.

It was the most amazing experience. We landed in Los Angeles where our coach collected us from and drove us down to San Diego. By the time we arrived, we had been up for almost thirty six hours!

We were very tired but on arriving at the hotel our adrenaline kicked in. Everything was so beautiful and so big.

We had an amazing time touring around Las Vegas, San Francisco, Los Angeles and many other wonderful places. We had such fun, but then we always do when we are together.

On our return, we were visited by our pastor who informed us that while we were away the elders had discussed starting healing rooms from out of our fellowship. This had been on their hearts for some time, but it was now that God gave the go ahead as it were.

They were told by the Lord to set us both aside to head up this ministry. I was glad I was sitting down, as the shock would have knocked me down.

We were given information about the healing rooms in London who were having a two-day training event. John and I went with one of the elders of our church. The main purpose was to find out about the healing rooms, as well as to see if John and I felt that this was something we felt the Lord was leading us into.

On the final day, the leaders of the course said they felt the Lord was telling them to do something they had never done before. They arranged two rows of chairs with a space down the middle. We had previously been talking about the river of God and they felt the Lord telling them that one by one we were to walk between the rows of chairs as if walking through a river.

We were sent into a back room while they prepared this. When we were called out, I was the first one to go. I was told to walk very slowly down the 'river' with my eyes closed. Kneeling on the seats were the team members blowing, and swooshing with their hands.

I started down very slowly. After only a few seconds, I was sobbing. I had no idea why except that the presence of God was so heavy, I had the feeling that if I stretched my hands out I would feel Him. In fact, that is exactly what did happen. When I got halfway down, I just had to stop. I was sobbing so much, and under my breath, I was telling the Lord that I was unequipped to take on healing rooms ministry and there was no way I could do it.

I then felt a hand take hold of my left hand. I thought it was one of the team members taking pity on me as I was by now reduced to a sobbing quivering wreck.

I opened my eyes very slightly just enough to peep through my eyelashes and I saw… the Lord… He was holding my hand and saying " child, you are not equipped but I AM " He was going to walk this journey with me. It would be Him who does it all. It had nothing at all to do with me!

That was the beginning of my journey into becoming addicted to His presence.

When I returned home the following day, I began telling people at my fellowship what I had just experienced. Some of the looks I received showed me that some people just did not get it. Nevertheless, some did and were encouraging. I so wanted the others to experience the same though.

The following weekend there was a two-day conference in Halifax where we could learn what the healing rooms were all about in more detail.

So, that weekend found us travelling to Halifax with our pastor, one of the other elders and a friend who just loved attending anything where the Holy Spirit was moving.

It was taken by Rick Taylor and his wife who had flown over from the States. They used to be at Bethel Church in Redding, California. I can't begin to describe the tangible presence of God in that place.

By the end of the second day, I had been well and

truly blitzed by the Holy Spirit. I was doubled over and groaning. What others now describe as 'Me having a baby!'

It was while we were at that conference that I met up with the lady who had led the previous weekend. She happened to be a regional director of the healing rooms and agreed to train me.

For the next six weeks, I travelled to London. I left very early on a Monday morning in order to attend one of her healing rooms to observe. I had to return at 7:30pm for the actual training. Once the morning sessions had finished, which, was around lunchtime I went to book into the only motel in the area, where I spent the afternoon just chilling out and waiting on the Lord. It was the seediest place I have ever stayed.

It was midsummer and hot! The motel did not have any air conditioning and the windows would not open. I stood it for as long as I could. I would then have a shower and leave early for the evening training just so I could go to the local Tesco store and stand in the freezer aisle to cool down! I do not 'do' heat very well.

The training was taken by an amazing anointed

woman, who stretched us in our ability to hear from God. The model for the healing rooms is for three people to be in the room praying for the client. She would call three of us out to the front to pray for a volunteer from her team. She would then tell us to get a word from the Lord for this person straight away.

It was a scary, amazing, awesome and fun time. I came away each week walking on cloud nine, because every week the Lord showed up, He never once let me down. The only fly in the ointment was that I had to return to the motel to sleep. I would then catch the train home the next morning.

On one particular night after I had turned the light out, I felt as if things were crawling all over me. It was driving me mad. I cried out to the Lord asking what it was. I then heard a small voice in my right ear. "They're bed bugs"

I was horrified. What was I going to do? Immediately I had said that, the answer came. Pray them off. I had never done anything like this before. However, I launched out and did just that. Within seconds, all the aggravation had stopped and I fell into a peaceful sleep. The next morning when I was sitting on the train reflecting on the previous night, I knew that the Lord had shown me through that ghastly experience just how He was going to walk with me.

It was a sad occasion when the final training day came. I had grown to love these people, and relished sitting under their anointing.

That night a lot of the team was present and the words that were spoken over those of us who had been training were awesome. The power of the Holy Spirit was so strong and tangible.

On returning home, we asked people at the church to give us their names if they felt the Lord was calling them into a healing ministry. We had twenty people come forward. We started training them in June and after eight weeks when it was finished they unanimously said that rather than break until October when we were due to open, they wanted to carry on meeting all through the summer!

God molded us together during that time, as we learnt to be completely transparent with each other. Each week the Holy Spirit met with us in different ways. It was a joyful, exciting, crazy and powerful experience.

October came and we opened our doors for the first time. I have to admit to being a little apprehensive. We had no idea who would come and what their condition would be.

I remember having a little panic when we had our first client suffering from cancer! Straight away Father whispered in my ear "headache – cancer, it is all the same for me".

While I was training, I heard about sending prayer cloths out to people who were unable to attend a healing room, and who had requested one. I immediately pooh-poohed the idea saying that was something we would not be doing!

This was before I heard a story about a little girl who was desperately ill. She lived in Australia and a prayer cloth had been requested from a healing room in America.

The leaders knew that time was of the essence, and if posted it would take an age to arrive. They photocopied the prayer cloth then faxed it to her parents. The parents then took the fax to the hospital and laid it on their daughter. She recovered!

That testimony certainly put me in my place. We send prayer cloths out to many countries, Canada, Australia and Spain to name a few and have received amazing testimonies from them. A lady healed of cancer, another lady dying of heart failure, chronic back pain healed, fibromyalgia healed and many more .I do not understand everything about healing. I do not understand fully about prayer cloths. However, I KNOW that God is faithful, He is the healer and when we walk in obedience to Him and His commands, and He heals and blesses people. That is good enough for me.

I used to watch people such as Benny Hinn on the God channel and pray longingly that I could be used like him. To see him praying for people and the power of God causing them to fall down right where they were. I wanted to have an anointing like that.

Years passed by but nothing seemed to happen. Nevertheless, since that day in London my life has never been the same. The joy that the Lord baptised me in has not left. I am on an amazing journey with the Lord.

A couple of weeks ago He gave me a picture,

which blew me away!

I was standing at the end of a path, but this path was covered in rocks, broken glass, and sharp flint and had thistles growing in from the sides. As I looked, I said to the Lord that there was no way I could walk down that path.

As soon as the words left my mouth, the Lord came from my left side and proceeded to walk down the path.

As He walked further into it, His feet started to bleed from all the glass and flint. His legs were cut and scratched from the brambles. The blood was fresh.

He turned to look at me and urged me to walk close behind Him as the brambles that He was treading on would soon grow up again, but if I stayed close, I would not get hurt. He was still taking all the pain for me.

This had such an impact on me. I had always known that He died and suffered in my place but sometimes although we know that, it seems to be way back then as it were. This picture brought everything into the present.

He IS still taking our pain. The image of walking so close behind Him is all the security we need.

It has taken me sixty years to get to the place I am now with God, but He told me that He could do more in one year with me now as I am than anything I alone could achieve in a decade. There is no retirement in the kingdom of God, and nobody is ever too old or past it.

There are times when I wonder what would have happened if I had not walked into disobedience and gone my own way for fifteen years.

However, God's grace and forgiveness overwhelms me. All I know is that I want to live the rest of my life for Him, making every day count.

EPILOGUE

What then is the purpose of my writing this book?

To show what God can do with a broken, nervous, insecure, abused little girl, who grew up to be a shy, insecure, sometimes controlling and manipulative woman.

The journey has not been easy, but neither was His.

The Healing Rooms have now been opened for two years, and it has been a privilege to see how God meets people week after week after week.

He not only touches their physical bodies, but reaches right down into their emotional need as well. People walk out knowing that they have been in His presence. That is what healing rooms is all about…..His Presence. Without Him, we can do nothing.

Is every day perfect? No…..but we have a loving

Savior who has given us the victory over the enemy and everything, he tries to throw at us. He walked that path of suffering for us that we might not have to. All we have to do is stay close to Him.

One of the most important things the Lord showed me was that I had to forgive my uncle and all the others who have abused me in one way or another.

Was that easy? No… I had to choose to do it. We must forgive as we have been forgiven.

His love is unconditional but His forgiveness is not.

Father has done amazing things in my life. John and I have the most amazing marriage. We have a wonderful family, which is growing all the time. We have eleven grandchildren.

We have wonderful brothers and sisters in the Lord. The Lord just goes on providing for us in every way.

I have read many autobiographies in the past, which have testified to many amazing things that God has done in their lives and I have always finished them saying, "yeah that's ok for them but it'll never happen to me!"

I am testifying today that it can happen to anybody!

All that is required is total surrender to God.

Hand Him the reins and let Him get on and do what He wants to do in your life.

There is nothing better on this earth than feeling free, secure, and more than anything…..loved, and accepted. The love God has for each of us is awesome **- and yes, that does include you!**

If you are interested in visiting the Healing Rooms, contact us on:

Tel: 07503 905702

Printed in Great Britain
by Amazon